What's in this book

This book belongs to

_____

保护动物 Protect the animals

学习内容 Contents

沟通 Communication

认出动物并说说它们
Identify animals and talk about them

生词 New words

★ 它们	they, them
★ 可爱	lovely
★ 身体	body
★ 胖	fat
★ 瘦	thin
★ 因为	because, because of
★ 所以	therefore
★ 牙	tooth
宠物	pet
金鱼	goldfish
斑马	zebra
象	elephant

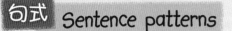

句式 Sentence patterns

因为小狗病了，所以它变瘦了。
The dog is getting thinner because it is sick.

因为动物是我们的朋友，所以我们要保护它们。
We have to protect animals because they are our friends.

跨学科学习 Project

地球上濒临绝种的动物
Earth's endangered animals

文化 Cultures

中西文化中龙的象征
The symbolic meanings of
dragons in Chinese and
Western cultures

Get ready

1 Where are the students going?

2 Why do you think some pets and animals live there?

3 How do you think we should treat pets and animals?

tā men kě ài ma
它们可爱吗？

"你们家里有宠物吗？它们可爱吗？"
老师问。

"我有金鱼。它有胖胖的身体、大大的眼睛。"爱莎说。

"我有小狗。因为它最近病了,所以它变瘦了。"浩浩说。

牙 yá

"这些斑马皮包和象牙盒子，你们会用吗？"老师问。

"我不用！我在动物园见过斑马。斑
马很可爱！"伊森说。

"因为动物是我们的朋友，所以我们
要保护它们。"伊森说。

Let's think

1 Recall the story. Put a tick or a cross.

2 What would you do if you saw a stray or disabled animal on the street? Discuss with your friend.

New words

1 Learn the new words.

因为　所以　身体　牙　象　斑马　宠物　可爱　胖　金鱼　它们　瘦

2 Listen to your friend and point to the correct words above.

 1 Listen and circle the mistakes.

 2 Look at the pictures. Listen to the story a

1

2

3

妈妈，因为小动物很可爱，所以我喜欢它们。

因为动物是我们的朋友，所以我们

J.

 这只小猫很胖，那只小狗很瘦。

这 它们很喜欢吃饼干。

护它们。

3 Complete the sentences. Write the letters and say.

a 多 b 胖 c 瘦 d 前

1

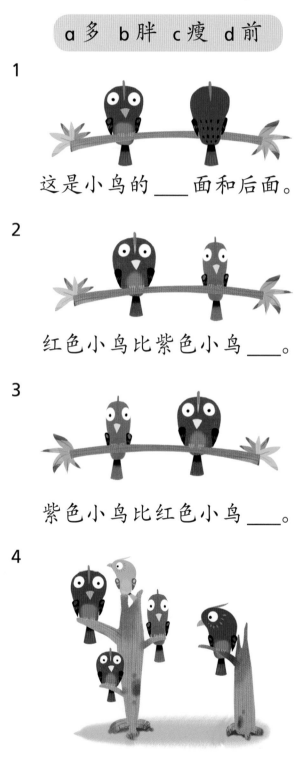

这是小鸟的 ___ 面和后面。

2

红色小鸟比紫色小鸟 ___。

3

紫色小鸟比红色小鸟 ___。

4

大树上面的小鸟 ___。

Task

Find out which animals
your classmates like.
Write the numbers.

动物	多少人喜欢？	多少人见过？
猫		
狗		
金鱼		
斑马		
大象		
熊猫		
老虎		

Game

Listen to your teacher and point to the correct pets.

艾文的宠物不见了。它
是一只胖胖的白色的大
狗。它在哪里？

小黄很胖，牙很
大。它的耳朵不
长。它在哪里？

Chant

 Listen and say.

我有一只大花猫，
它有白色的毛毛，
身体胖胖像个包。
我有一只大黄狗，
它有黑色的眼睛，
身体胖胖像个球。
我们喜欢猫和狗，
大家都是好朋友。

生活用语 Daily expressions

小心！
Be careful!

不小心。
Careless.

写一写 Write

1 Trace and write the characters.

丨 冂 冃 囙 囝 因

丶 ソ 为 为

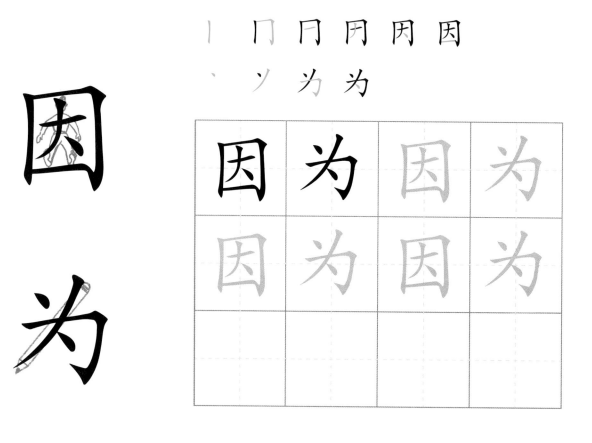

因	为	因	为
因	为	因	为

2 Write and say.

_____ 它吃了很多，所以它的身体胖胖的。

_____ 它病了，所以它不高兴。

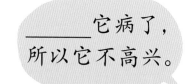

16

3 Fill in the blanks with the correct words.
Colour in the paws using the same colours.

岁

因为

它

___叫布朗尼。___今年三___了。_____很喜欢吃，所以___胖胖的。

朋友们喜欢___，_____很可爱。我也爱我的宠物。

Choose the correct pictures for the input methods. Write the letters.

Phonetic-based method ⬜

Shape-based method ⬜

There are two methods to write Chinese on a computer. The phonetic-based method allows pronunciations to be converted into characters. The shape-based method is based on the structure of the characters.

a

b

多元学习 Connections

Cultures

1. The dragon is an ancient mythical creature in both Eastern and Western cultures. Which dragon do you like?

The Chinese dragon is a symbol of power, strength and good luck for people. It is also the imperial symbol of the Emperors of China.

The Western dragon is a legendary and mythical creature. It is aggressive and warlike. Its blood often contains magical powers.

2. Help the knight find the right dragon head. Circle it.

哪一个头是它的呢？

Project

1 There are many reasons why there are endangered animals. Learn about them.

Hunting

Natural disaster

Pollution

Food chain

Migration

Drought

2 Match the animals to the correct locations. Discuss with your friend why these animals are endangered.

a 老虎　　b 熊猫　　c 大象

因为可爱的动物变少了，所以我们要保护它们。

温习 Checkpoint

1 Complete the tasks to play the puzzle game.
Write the numbers in the boxes.

1 Say 'It is very thin.' in Chinese.

2 What is the opposite of '瘦'?

3 大象真可爱。

它们是什么动物? Answer in Chinese.

4 Why should we protect the animals? Answer in Chinese.

金鱼的身体胖胖的。

Write 'because' in Chinese.

5 因为它吃了很多，所以它胖了。

8 Say 'My pet has 16 teeth.' in Chinese.

2 Work with your friend. Colour the stars and the chillies.

Words	说	读	写
它们	☆	☆	🌶
可爱	☆	☆	🌶
身体	☆	☆	🌶
胖	☆	☆	🌶
瘦	☆	☆	🌶
因为	☆	☆	☆
所以	☆	☆	🌶
牙	☆	☆	🌶
宠物	☆	🌶	🌶
金鱼	☆	🌶	🌶

Words and sentences	说	读	写
斑马	☆	🌶	🌶
象	☆	🌶	🌶
因为小狗病了，所以它变瘦了。	☆	🌶	🌶
因为动物是我们的朋友，所以我们要保护它们。	☆	🌶	🌶

Identify animals and talk about them	☆

3 What does your teacher say?

My teacher says ...

21

分享 Sharing

Words I remember

它们	tā men	they, them
可爱	kě ài	lovely
身体	shēn tǐ	body
胖	pàng	fat
瘦	shòu	thin
因为	yīn wèi	because, because of
所以	suǒ yǐ	therefore
牙	yá	tooth
宠物	chǒng wù	pet
金鱼	jīn yú	goldfish
斑马	bān mǎ	zebra
象	xiàng	elephant

Other words

问	wèn	to ask
最近	zuì jìn	recently
病	bìng	to fall ill
变	biàn	to become
这些	zhè xiē	these
皮包	pí bāo	leather bag
盒子	hé zi	box
会	huì	to be likely to
用	yòng	to use
过	guò	(auxiliary word of tense)
要	yào	must
保护	bǎo hù	to protect
猫	māo	cat

OXFORD
UNIVERSITY PRESS

Oxford University Press is a department of the University of Oxford.
It furthers the University's objective of excellence in research, scholarship,
and education by publishing worldwide. Oxford is a registered trade mark of
Oxford University Press in the UK and in certain other countries

Published in Hong Kong by
Oxford University Press (China) Limited
39th Floor, One Kowloon, 1 Wang Yuen Street, Kowloon Bay,
Hong Kong

Illustrated by Anne Lee, Emily Chan, KK Ng, KY Chan and Wildman

Photographs for reproduction permitted by Dreamstime.com

China National Publications Import & Export (Group) Corporation is an authorized distributor of
Oxford Elementary Chinese.

Please contact content@cnpiec.com.cn or 86-10-65856782

ISBN: 978-0-19-942994-3

10 9 8 7 6 5 4 3 2